# Lost at
# School

Written by Monica Hughes

Illustrated by Julie Park

Lizzie and Dad went to the school fair.

They went to see Sam and Adam.

Lizzie went on the bouncy castle.

Lizzie went on the train.

She went to see the face painting.

Then Dad and Lizzie saw
Grandad and Rosie.

Grandad was busy.
Everybody wanted a balloon.

Dad wanted to help Grandad.

Then Dad looked for Lizzie but
Lizzie had gone.

'Lizzie has gone,' said Dad.

Dad looked for Lizzie on the train.

Mum looked for Lizzie on the bouncy castle.

Sam and Adam ran to the
face painting and . . .

Lizzie was there.